MATH ACTIVITIES

# FUN WITH DIVISION

Lorenzo McLellan
Illustrated by Natasha Rimmington

I0808965

WINDMILL BOOKS

Published in 2020 by Windmill Books,
an Imprint of Rosen Publishing
29 East 21st Street, New York, NY 10010



Written by Lorenzo McLellan
Illustrated by Natasha Rimmington
Designed by Well Nice, Elaine Wilkinson
Edited by Sebastian Rydberg, Julia Adams

Cataloging-in-Publication Data

Names: McLellan, Lorenzo.
Title: Fun with division / Lorenzo McLellan.
Description: New York : Windmill Books, 2020. | Series: Math activities
Identifiers: ISBN 9781725395275 (pbk.) | ISBN 9781725395299 (library bound) | ISBN 9781725395282 (6 pack)
Subjects: LCSH: Division–Juvenile literature. | Arithmetic–Juvenile literature.
Classification: LCC QA115.M354 2020 | DDC 513.2'14–dc23

Manufactured in the United States of America

CPSIA Compliance Information: Batch BS20WM: For Further Information contact Rosen Publishing, New York, New York at 1-800-237-9932

# How to Use This Book

Welcome to the world of Math Activities! This book is filled with great tips and facts to help you learn the basics of dividing—all while having fun! Grab a pencil and some paper so you can write down all your answers...then check your work on pages 30 and 31.

Read about each new topic before you dive into the activities.

Test your knowledge with exciting activities throughout.

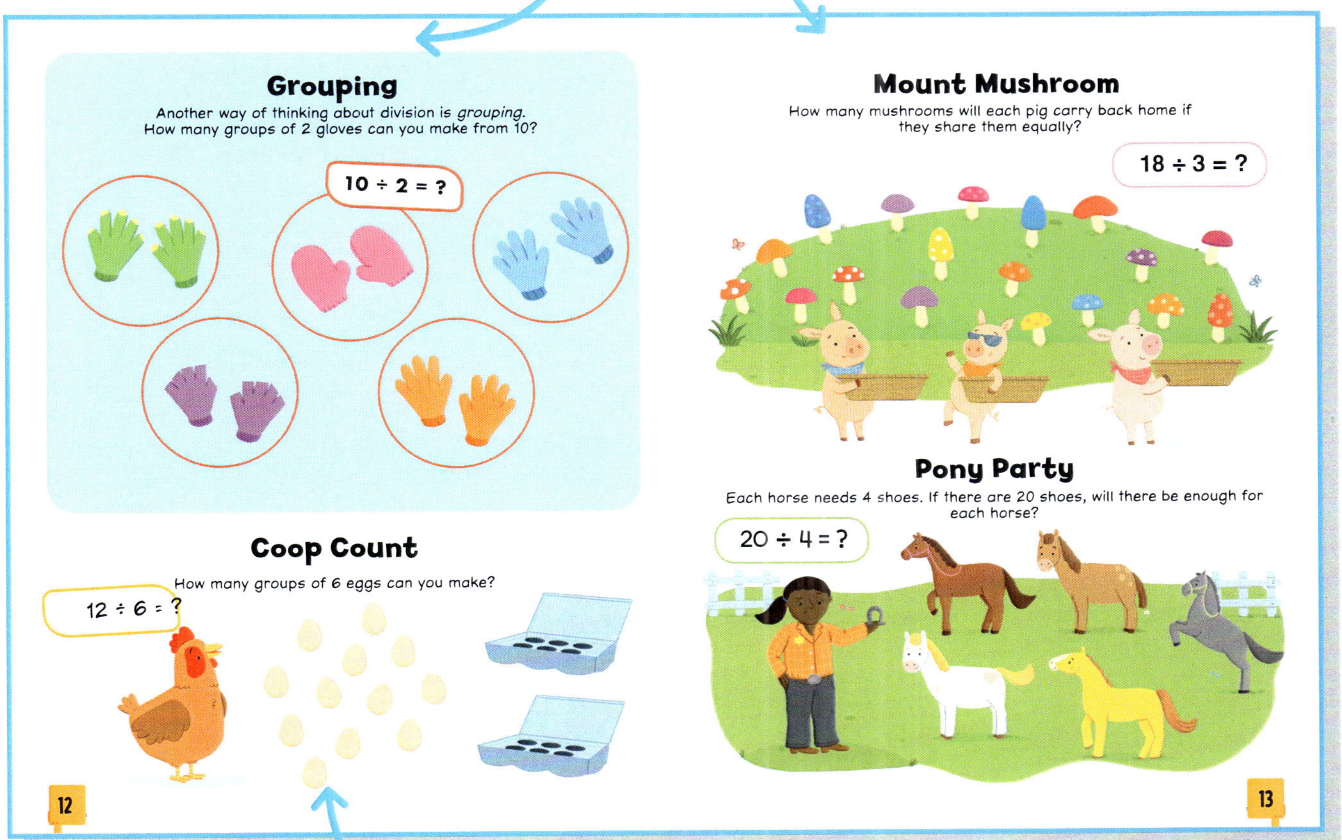


All new topics come with practice activities to learn key skills.

**Top Tip**

You may find it helpful to refer to the times tables while working on the activities.

# Learn the Symbols ( ÷ = )

To start dividing, these are the symbols you'll need to know.

÷ "DIVIDED BY" OR "GROUPING"

= "IS EQUAL TO"

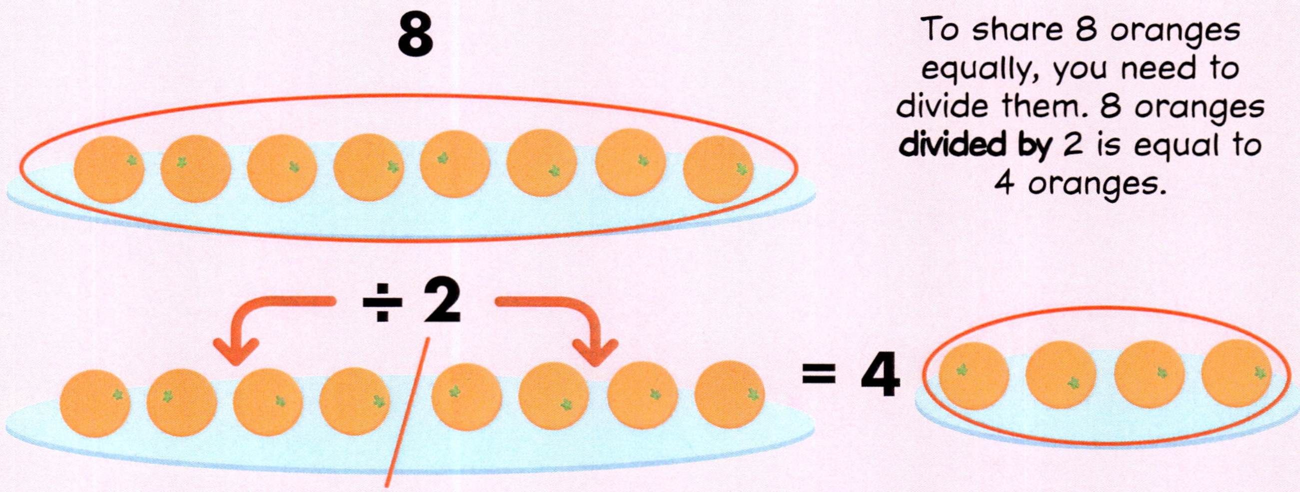


To share 8 oranges equally, you need to divide them. 8 oranges **divided by** 2 is equal to 4 oranges.

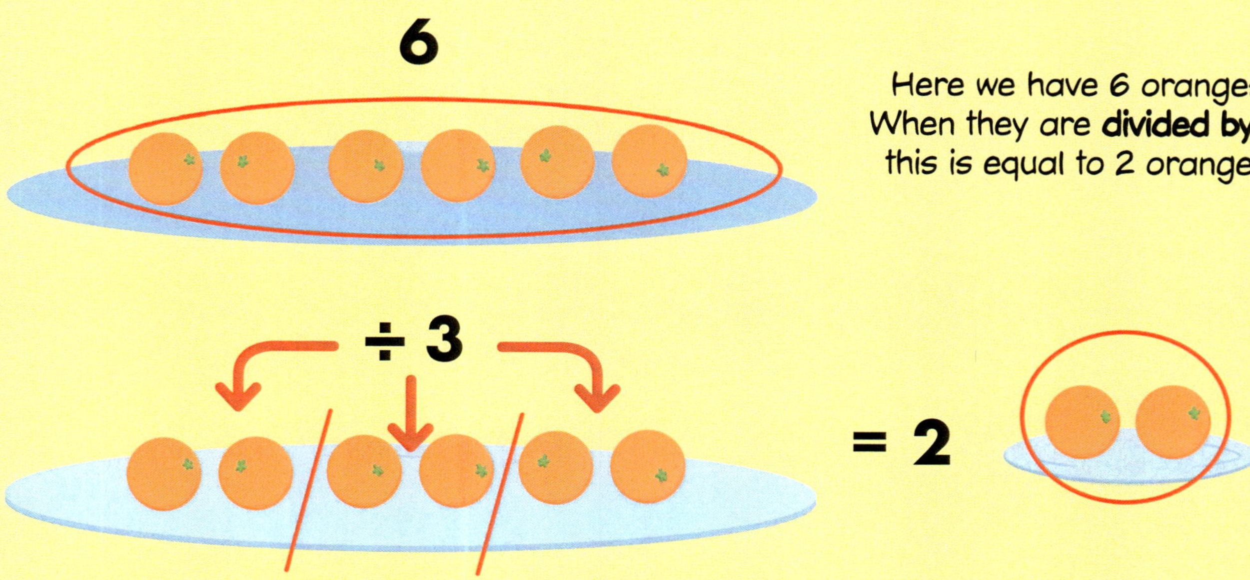


Here we have 6 oranges. When they are **divided by** 3, this is equal to 2 oranges.

# Sharing

We can think of division as sharing an amount into equal groups.

10 ÷ 5 = ?

Let's share 10 apples into 5 bowls equally. We can move each apple one by one until we have used all the apples. How many apples are there in each bowl/ equal group?

10 ÷ 5 = 2

# Banana Split

How many bananas does each monkey get?

6 ÷ 2 = ?

# Cavalry Crevasse

How many horses are on each side of the crack?

$$12 \div 2 = ?$$

# Jail Run

How many robbers will end up in each jail?

$$15 \div 3 = ?$$

# Mermaids' Treasure

Share the jewels out equally between each mermaid.
How many does each one get?

$$15 \div 5 = ?$$

# Beakfast!

How many worms does each chick get for breakfast?

$$8 \div 4 = ?$$

# Working Out the Inverse

Division and multiplication are the opposites of each other. One way of saying this is that they are *inverse* of each other. You can have fun figuring out the inverse of number sentences.

$5 \times 3 = 15$ $\quad$ $15 \div 3 = 5$

$3 \times 5 = 15$ $\quad$ $15 \div 5 = 3$

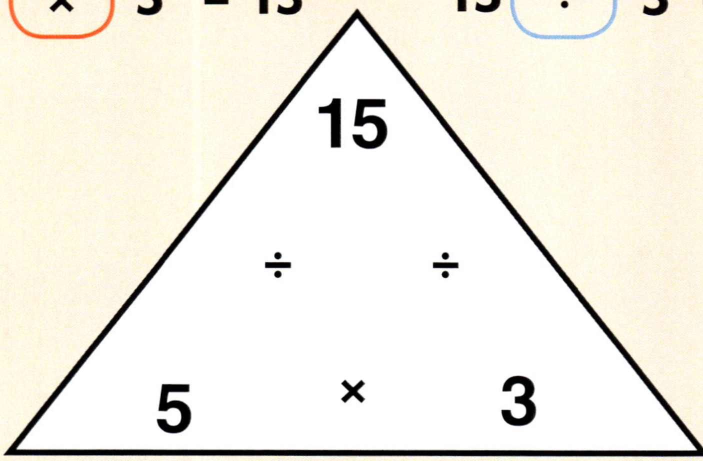

## Pyramid Puzzle

Use the Super Inverse Triangle inside the pyramid to help you fill in the gaps!

$3 \times 2 = 6$ $\quad$ $6 \div 3 = 2$

$2 \times ? = 6$ $\quad$ $6 \div 2 = ?$

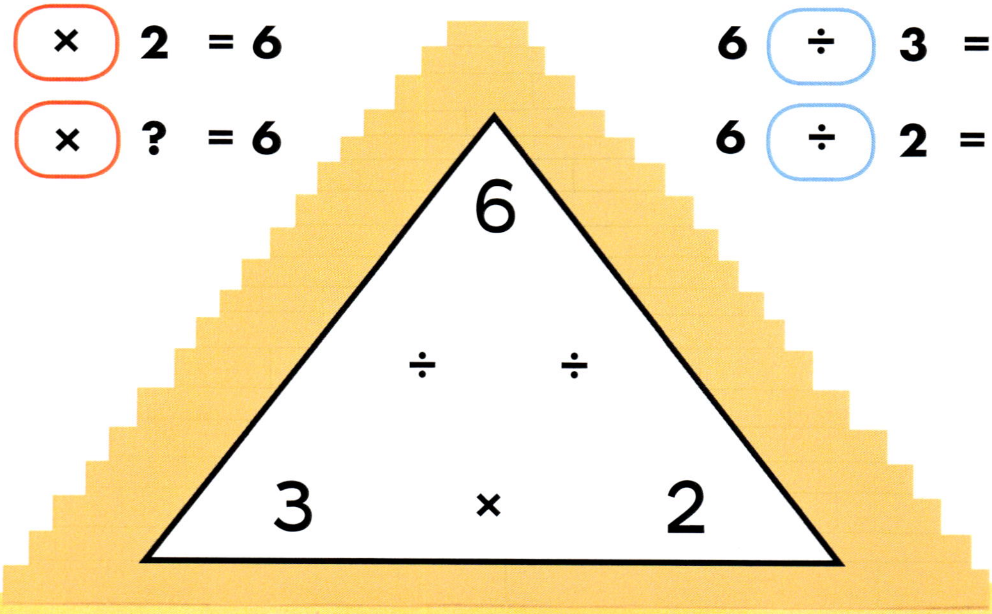

# Goblin Gold

Share the coins equally among the goblins. Can you write the two inverse equations? Use the Super Inverse Triangle to help you.

**20 ÷ 5 = ?**

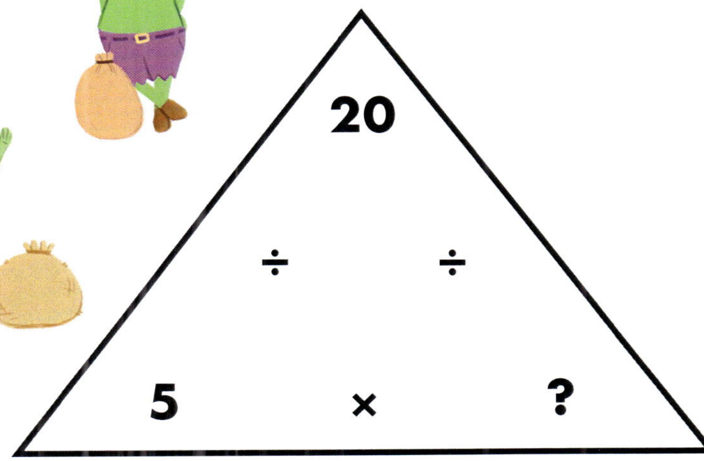


**1) 5 × ? = 20**

**2) ? × 5 = 20**

# Treetop Tightrope

Which rope leads the monkey to the correct inverse number sentence?

# Odd and Even Numbers

With **even** numbers, you can always share them out equally between two groups. With **odd** numbers, one group always gets more and one always gets less!

# All Aboard

Figure out if the number of penguins waiting to board the two boats is odd or even.

## Spring Cleaning

Help the fairy tidy up all the numbers into the right boxes by writing down which numbers are odd and which ones are even.

## Odd Dinner

Which clown is the odd one out?

# Grouping

Another way of thinking about division is *grouping*. How many groups of 2 gloves can you make from 10?

# Coop Count

How many groups of 6 eggs can you count?

# Mount Mushroom

How many mushrooms will each pig carry back home
if they share them equally?

$18 \div 3 = ?$

# Pony Party

Each horse needs 4 shoes. If there are 20 shoes, will there
be enough for each horse?

$20 \div 4 = ?$

# Wild Goose Race

Help the goose get to the finish line by tracing the correct path with your finger!

# Market Mix-up

Match the total of each number sentence to the correct food.

# Honeycomb Hunt

Which segment is missing?

# Boar-thday Cake

How many slices of cake will each boar get? Complete the number sentence below.

6 ÷ ? = ?

# Friends from Afar

What are the aliens trying to say to you? Find the solutions and use the key to figure it out.

1) 20 ÷ 5 = ?
2) 33 ÷ 3 = ?
3) 63 ÷ 9 = ?
4) 35 ÷ 7 = ?
5) 10 ÷ 1 = ?

KEY

| | | |
|---|---|---|
| 11 = U | 81 = D | 25 = B |
| 5 = C | 7 = R | 10 = K |
| 4 = O | 90 = Y | |

# Test Your Knowledge

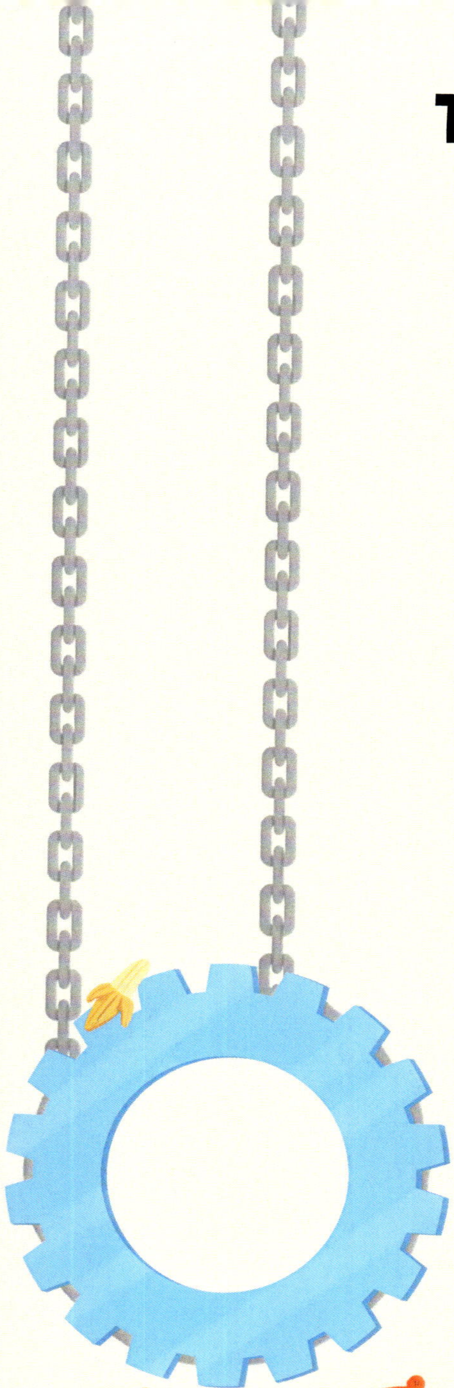

1) 6 ÷ 3 = ?

2) 18 ÷ 3 = ?

3) 7 ÷ 7 = ?

4) 49 ÷ 7 = ?

5) 16 ÷ 4 = ?

6) 12 ÷ 4 = ?

7) 20 ÷ 4 = ?

8) 4 ÷ 2 = ?

9) 30 ÷ 5 = ?

10) 24 ÷ 6 = ?

# Test Your Knowledge

1) Find the odd numbers: 12 33 54 2 91

2) Find the even numbers: 21 11 32 1,000

3) $40 \div 5 =$ ?

4) $45 \div 9 =$ ?

5) $20 \div 5 =$ ?

6) $90 \div 9 =$ ?

7) $24 \div 3 =$ ?

8) $28 \div 7 =$ ?

9) $54 \div 6 =$ ?

10) $9 = 81 \div$ ?

# Showtime

Help the clown get to the stage in time for the show.
Trace the correct path with your finger!

# Hop to It!

Help each frog find its lily pad.

# Number Machine

Rewrite each division problem by swapping around the numbers before and after each "is equal to" sign.

# Creepy Crawly Maze

Help the worm get to his friends by tracing the safe path with your finger.

# Market Mix-up

Which bag has the wrong number of oranges?

$33 \div 3 = 11$

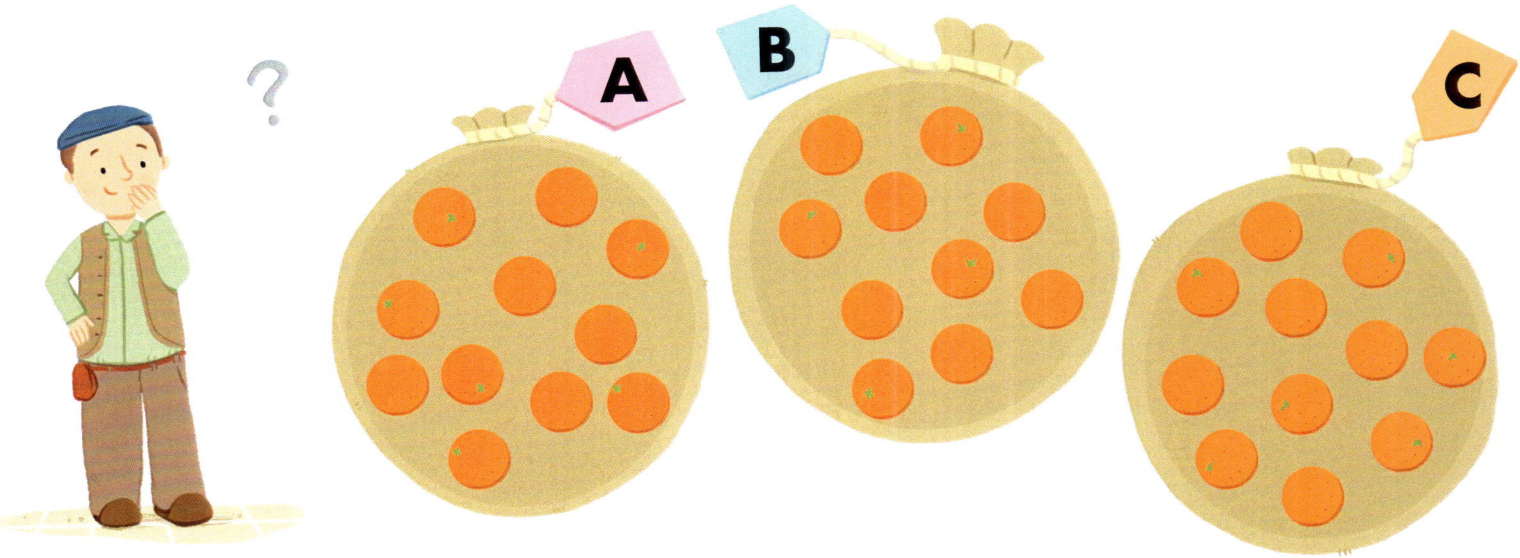


# Lineup

Pick the guilty robber!

$108 \div 9 =$

# Robo-road

Help the robot collect the tools and get back to his friends. Use your finger, and only pick roads that can be divided by 4 or 8.

# Underwater Wonderland

What are the fish trying to say?
Clue: Not all the letters in the key are needed!

★ N ★ E ★    ★ ★ E    ★ E ★
1   2   3    4 5    6   7

1) $12 \div 4 =$ ?

2) $30 \div 5 =$ ?

3) $70 \div 10 =$ ?

4) $16 \div 2 =$ ?

5) $24 \div 6 =$ ?

6) $36 \div 4 =$ ?

7) $90 \div 9 =$ ?

KEY

| | | | | |
|---|---|---|---|---|
| 11 = P | 5 = Y | 4 = H | 10 = A | 6 = D |
| 2 = K | 8 = T | 9 = S | 7 = R | 3 = U |

# Test Your Knowledge

1) $36 \div 6 =$ ?

2) $30 \div 5 =$ ?

3) $60 \div 10 =$ ?

4) $16 \div 4 =$ ?

5) $8 \div 2 =$ ?

6) $32 \div 8 =$ ?

7) $24 \div 12 =$ ?

8) $12 \div 2 =$ ?

9) $6 \div 3 =$ ?

10) $15 \div 3 =$ ?

# Test Your Knowledge

1) 36 ÷ 12 = ?

2) 10 ÷ 1 = ?

3) 42 ÷ 6 = ?

4) 21 ÷ 7 = ?

5) 36 ÷ 9 = ?

6) 70 ÷ 10 = ?

7) 55 ÷ 5 = ?

8) 48 ÷ 4 = ?

9) 48 ÷ 8 = ?

10) 99 ÷ 11 = ?

# Test Your Knowledge

1) Miss Tunch shares 20 chocolates equally among 5 children. How many chocolates does each child get?

2) 10 coins are split equally into 5 bags. How many coins are in each bag?

3) 24 animals need to be split into groups of 2. How many groups of 2 will there be?

4) 20 zappers need to be shared among 10 aliens. How many zappers does each alien receive?

5) There are 36 reindeer and 6 sleighs. How many reindeer does each sleigh get?

# Test Your Knowledge

1) 30 children split into 3 equal teams. How many children will be in each team?

2) There are 4 cats that each have the same amount of kittens. There are 20 kittens. How many kittens does each cat have?

3) A wizard sorts his 15 wands into 5 drawers. How many wands will end up in each drawer?

4) There are 4 buses for a school trip. Each bus can take 6 children, and there are 24 children who would like to take part in the trip. Will there be enough space for all of them on the buses?

5) There are 7 pirates who discover a treasure chest with 42 rubies. How many rubies does each pirate get if they share them equally?

# Solutions

**Page 5**

6 ÷ 2 = 3

**Page 6**

12 ÷ 2 = 6

**Page 6**

15 ÷ 3 = 5

**Page 7**

15 ÷ 5 = 3

**Page 7**

8 ÷ 4 = 2

**Page 8**

2 × 3 = 6

6 ÷ 2 = 3

**Page 9**

20 ÷ 5 = 4

1) 5 × 4 = 20

2) 4 × 5 = 20

**Page 9**

15 ÷ 3 = 5

**Page 10**

1) 4 is even

2) 5 is odd

**Page 10**

11 is odd

**Page 11**

**Page 11**

**Page 12**

10 ÷ 2 = 5

**Page 12**

12 ÷ 6 = 2

**Page 13**

18 ÷ 3 = 6

**Page 13**

20 ÷ 4 = 5

**Page 14**

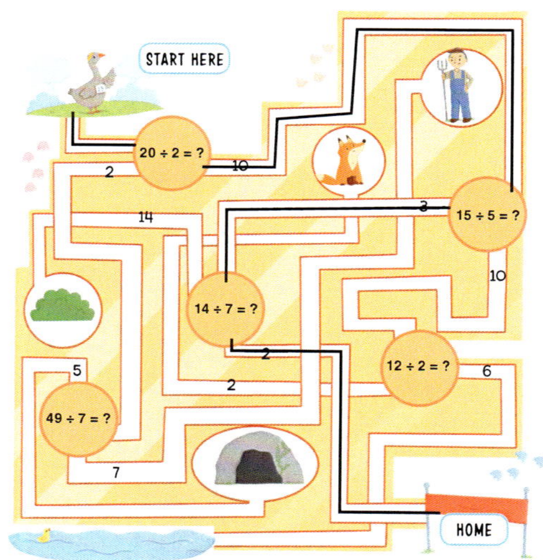


**Page 15**

**Page 15**

**Page 16**

6 ÷ (3) = (2)

**Page 17**

YOU ROCK!

1) 20 ÷ 5 = 4

2) 33 ÷ 3 = 11

3) 63 ÷ 9 = 7

4) 35 ÷ 7 = 5

5) 10 ÷ 1 = 10

**Page 18**

| | |
|---|---|
| 1) 2 | 6) 3 |
| 2) 6 | 7) 5 |
| 3) 1 | 8) 2 |
| 4) 7 | 9) 6 |
| 5) 4 | 10) 4 |

# Solutions

**Page 19**

1) 33; 91
2) 32; 1,000
3) 8
4) 5
5) 4
6) 10
7) 8
8) 4
9) 9
10) 9

**Page 20**

**Page 21**

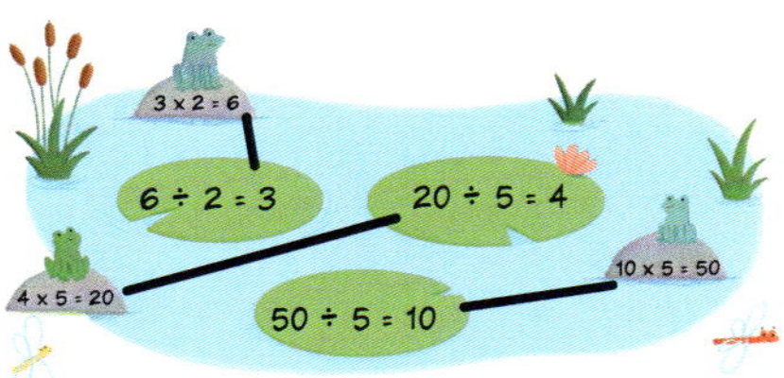


**Page 21**

1) 12 ÷ 4 = 3
2) 14 ÷ 2 = 7
3) 30 ÷ 6 = 5

**Page 22**

**Page 23**

B has only 10 oranges

**Page 23**

Robber C
108 ÷ 9 = 12

**Page 24**

**Page 25**

UNDER THE SEA

1) 12 ÷ 4 = 3
2) 30 ÷ 5 = 6
3) 70 ÷ 10 = 7
4) 16 ÷ 2 = 8
5) 24 ÷ 6 = 4
6) 36 ÷ 4 = 9
7) 90 ÷ 9 = 10

**Page 26**

1) 6
2) 6
3) 6
4) 4
5) 4
6) 4
7) 2
8) 6
9) 2
10) 5

**Page 27**

1) 3
2) 10
3) 7
4) 3
5) 4
6) 7
7) 11
8) 12
9) 6
10) 9

**Page 28**

1) 4
2) 2
3) 12
4) 2
5) 6

**Page 29**

1) 10
2) 5
3) 3
4) Yes: 24 ÷ 4 = 6
5) 6

# Glossary

**even number** An even number is one that you can divide by 2, with no remainder.

**inverse** To be the opposite of something. For example, division is the inverse of multiplication.

**multiplication** To multiply a number is the same as adding that number again and again: 3 x 2 is the same as 2 + 2 + 2.

**odd number** An odd number is one that you can't divide evenly by 2.

**Super Inverse Triangle** An arrangement of math symbols and numbers in a triangle that can help you figure out inverse equations.

# Further Information


Rogers, Kirsteen, Tori Large et al. *Usborne Elementary Illustrated Math Dictionary.* London, UK: Usborne Publishing, 2010.

Vorderman, Carol. *Times Tables Made Easy.* London, UK: DK Publishing, 2012.


# Index